The Breaking

& Shaking in

Sisterhood

SOPHIA LONG

ISBN: 978-1-63848-888-0

ACKNOWLEDGEMENTS

First and foremost, I continuously "THANK GOD" for my "Beginning" and "Ending" of how my story began in my "Life." Whoever would of thought I'd know "GOD" this way? "God" is my "HEALER," my "CONFIDONT," He's all that, plus some to me. If it hadn't been for the "LORD" who was on my side, tell me where would I be? "GOD" is such an "AMAZING" friend—all that I could ever want in anyone! I realized that it was Him from the start—God has always carried me through the "Storm" and the "RAIN." "I LOVE" "GOD" for allowing me to share my story time and time again, to experience things personally, and now sharing openly. "GOD," you're so "AMAZING"—that you are!

I also want to "THANK GOD" for the "MOST" "Amazing" "Woman" that there is on earth—my "MOTHER"! "MOTHER," I want to "THANK YOU" so much for "NEVER" giving up and "THROWING" away the "TOWEL" on me. I'm sorry for the "HEARTACHE" and "PAIN" I've caused, along with many "SLEEPLESS" nights! Most of all, "THANK YOU" for "PRAYING" for me. "Thank you" "Mother" for the "FEET" you had to put down on me in order for me to feel your "PAIN" and become the "WOMAN" you've always wanted me to be. "THANK YOU" "MOTHER" for showing me your "STRENGTH" and what it means to "STAND" on your own two feet! I "Thank you" "Mother" for carrying me in your "WOMB" when there were other options, which could have caused you to abandon me; but "GOD" saw fit for you to deal with someone like me! "I LOVE YOU MOTHER"!

I also want to "Thank God" for my five "BEAUTIFUL" children He has given me: "TYRON," "TYSHAWN," TYVONTAE," TYRE," and "TERI'YANA," in order to remind me of why I'm still striving in this world today! "MOMMA" love you all! I "Thank God" for those that has been on their "Hands and Knees" talking about "GOD" on my behalf! …those that have been "Pure", I want to say "THANK YOU"! "Thanks" to everyone that have been a "GREAT" "Blessing" and "IMPACT" in my "LIFE" that's now with the "LORD" "GOD", "THANK YOU" for the times we've shared! "I miss and "LOVE" you all "DEARLY," please continue to keep a "Watchful" eye over me and my children! "Thanks" to the person that has taken the time to "Edit" and help "Publish" my story! "THANK YOU" for all the "HARD WORK" and time spent on the last few books!

I also want to "Thank" those that have been in my "LIFE" in and out of season! I truly miss and "LOVE" you all!

I "LOVE" all of you, my "Family" no matter what! To everyone I know and don't know personally, "I LOVE YOU" as well! "Thanks" to all those that have been following me, and sowing into my "LIFE" as well! Thank you to all those that have been "TRULY" a "BLESSING" to me and my children! "THANK YOU" from the "BOTTOM" of my "HEART"! "I LOVE YOU ALL"! Please continue to be a "BLESSING" by sharing!! To "LOVE" is to "SHARE," and "PRAY," and be "KIND" to one another! Keep on "PUSHING" and "PRESSING" on, and know "GOD" got you!

Table Of Contents

The Breaking

& Shaking in

Sisterhood

CHAPTER 1

THE BROKENNESS

Many people have no clue what it "TRULY" means to "EMBRACE" a "Sister"! We're "BUSY" knocking each other down with our words, and ignoring one another with the same pain we all have in common. "Most" "Women" just don't know how to even keep it "REAL"; so they cover up their pain as if they're not the main ones crying—soaking their pillows in tears. But still and yet, you have people using your situation against you, as if they're "NOT" battling the same "Struggles" you're facing. The feeling of being alone, and being "HURT" and "PLAYED" by a "MAN"…

Let's not "FORGET", "MOST" of us "WOMEN" are raising our children alone. Let's be "HONEST", "WIVES"— you may even have a "CHEATING"-ass-"HUSBAND" at home, or better yet, he got you, and a whole family on the side!

1

"O", "Sophia" being too "REAL"; but it's "O.K."—I'll keep going!

You have the "NERVE" to act as if your "ASS" don't "STANK", as you're pretending to act as if everything is so perfect in your "BROKEN" marriage. …walking around like its ok to "JUDGE" the next "WOMEN", as if your situation is "Better" than hers. There's too many "WOMEN" that's "Broken" out here because of "NEGATIVE" conversations that's "BREAKING" other "WOMEN" down. How does "SOPHIA" know? She's one of them; so "LIFE" isn't a game until you lose "WOMEN" that meant a lot to you, those you held "DEARLY" to your heart.

"Sophia" don't have time for just talking and dealing with "WOMEN" that's "NEGATIVE" and "STAGNANT". Where they do that at? It's like wasting time when there's too many "WOMEN" hurting that will appreciate your "LOVE" and "KINDNESS." "Sophia" brings a different "LIGHT" and "Perspective" to the "LIVES" of many people. That's why "GOD" uses her to connect with many "Women" that have experienced different walks of life!

"Sophia" knows what it feels like to be in your shoes, and if she don't, she would just listen to you in order for you to release the "Pain" you're feeling. "Sophia" knows what it feels like to be "REJECTED" and "Overlooked"—that's why she can relate to you, you, and you. "Sophia" don't like when her time is being wasted because that could have been time used on helping another "LIFE", she could have spent her time with someone else. Of course, she enjoys the journey—sharing her "LIFE" with other people!

What don't kill you will makes you "Stronger." A lot of times the "MOST" "Broken" people are the ones that are "OVERLOOKED". …it's only because of the "POWER" you carry on the inside. No need to "BRAG" on who you are when you know the "STRENGTH" you carry! When a person has their "Purpose" that live on the inside of them, people tend to twist the "WRONG" things up concerning you. The world would be in such a "GREAT" place if people can be "TRUE" to themself.

Why were "Women" born "Women"? …not to be "JEALOUS" and cause the next sister harm because you're mad or "JEALOUS" at her outcome. "Women" are born "Women" to "EMPOWER" the next "Woman." "Women" are born "Nurturers" in order to show "Compassion" to other people. It should not be about "Competing" and who's trying to get ahead. That's what's wrong with many people in the black communities. Everyone wants to get ahead and show people who they are; but if you really sit back and observe those that flash things on social media (what they have today), those are the ones that didn't grow up having many things— they grew up in a "Broken" home.

"Women" we "MUST" do better in the things we do when raising our children and the company we keep around our children. Everyone isn't who we think they are. We need to "STOP" being so desperate for a "MAN" and use that same energy in "GOD", so He can fill the "VOID" in our "LIFE." There's no need to try and put the next "WOMAN" down when you're dealing with the same "PAIN" she's dealing with on the inside, and facing the same secret battles she's enduring. That other "WOMEN" is afraid just as well as you are. She doesn't want to share her personal information of struggles because she can't "TRUST" anyone, just as well as you.

"Women" we "MUST" do "BETTER" when we're so quick to "JUDGE" the next; and as "QUIET" as kept, that same "WOMAN" you're silently "HATING", her heart is "BLEEDING" as well! The same "WOMEN" you're "HATING" on had to "ENCOURAGE" herself to keep her "HEAD" above water as well! The same "WOMEN" you're laughing at had to stand in long lines at food pantries to make sure she had food for her children as well as you. So "LADIES", how "BROKEN" are you and where do you really stand? How long are you going to keep pretending you're your

"LIFE" is ok—and you're "Bleeding" deeply on the inside.
What will it take for you to "LOVE" the next "WOMAN" that
"STANDS" beside you?

"O" "MY" "GOD" Sophia can't "STAND" when
"BROKEN'' "Women" sees the next "BROKEN" "Woman"
and her "STRUGGLES" show on the outside along with her
children. ...AND many of you "WOMEN" just "LAUGH"
and talk about how dirty her and her children are. Where do
they do that at? Who are you representing? When you do such
a thing? "Please" don't tell me you're one of the people that
says they "LOVE" "GOD" and do such a thing; because
"SOPHIA" clearly don't see "SHIT" funny on that note!
"Women" we "MUST" do better, and if you ever been in a
"TOUGH" situation you know what I mean, especially if
you're someone that "WON'T" "FORGET" where you come
from!

It's time to do "BETTER"! If you don't "LEAD" by an
example for your children, remember you're just leading on
another "BROKEN" generation behind you. Somebody has to
set the right example to their children and their children's
children so as to leave behind a "GREAT" legacy. Somebody
has to bring back "BIG-MOMMA" and "Grandmom" back into
their family. Whose "PRAYING"? Whose being the leader in

the family? Whose going to be the one to be the "Strong" one? Who's the glue? Who is the person that people can go to for "POSITIVITY"?

Whose leading you? Come on "WOMEN", we have to be the glue, we need to "PRAY" for the "'MEN", we need the "GRANDFATHERS" to come back in this generation. How safe do you really feel if your time was up today or tomorrow? Do you know if your children and family would be "Spiritually" equipped to "STAND" on their own two feet? Or would you leave them to the "WORLD"—with all types of "DEMONS" that's rolling around to eat up our children flesh.

Come on "'WOMEN", do your children know a few scriptures or two? Ask yourself will your child be able to survive without the knowledge of the "WORD", using carnal knowledge and the street slang? "We got to use what we got in order to get what you want." Come on that's "PLAYED" out, and where did that get you in "LIFE"? How far did you go? Where did you end up? How much have you accomplished? "Sophia" is being too "REAL," but it's the "TRUTH"! Most "WOMEN" still holding on to "Childhood" pain and brought it into their adulthood. How is that working out for you?

You have to "FORGIVE" and "FORGET" what "JOHNNY" and your "DADDY" did to you! "YES" it "HURTS" like "HELL," but you have to let it go! It's not for

6

them, it's for you! Those that "HURT" you have moved on in their "LIFE," and you still holding on! It's time to give it to "GOD". So what if you have to seek counseling, so did "Sophia"! "Life" isn't easy, but I promise if you allow "GOD" in to show you and give you understanding of why you had to go through the "HELL" you've gone through, you'll be a whole different you! "GOD" is trying to get your attention.

"Women" we're "STRONGER" than we think! I know when that "MAN" you "TRUSTED" "BETRAYED" you, it cut you so "DEEPLY" it made you feel like you were all alone; and "GUESS" what, there's "MILLIONS" of "Women" who know what that same "PAIN" feels like. It may be a different story (who knows); but "PAIN" is "PAIN". So why should we be "BITTER" towards the next "WOMEN"!? Why should you want to fight the "Woman" that slept with the "MAN" that "HURT" you? No pain is no greater! We all know what it feels like to have our hearts bleed.

You have some "Women" that have similar stories of knowing how it feels to be "Molested," "Rejected," Misused," "Mistreated," "Abandoned," and last not least, one of "MOST" "POPULAR" subject—"Raising children" alone. A lot of "PAIN" comes from our childhood, and we confide in a

"MAN" as if he's our everything when he's not! "LOL", "TRUST", "Sophia" is being "HONEST"!

We can try everything in this world if you want, and still "NOT" be "HAPPY". "Hey", some of us even tried other "WOMEN", can I be "HONEST"? "Sophia" sure can "VOCHUE" on that one ("LOL"), and "GUESS" what—she was still "HURT" and "WOUNDED" from her "PAST" pain. She "NEVER" took time out to face and see why she was so "ANGRY" and why she became "BITTER" because she didn't want to face her own demons.

If you "NEVER" take the time out to look at yourself in the mirror and face what's on the inside of you you'll "NEVER" understand the next persons pain. It's ok to have time to be alone and "LOVE" on you! How can you "LOVE" someone else if you don't "LOVE" yourself? How does that work? "LOL," we can be a "MESS" and still put ourselves in a "DEEPER" mess, then "BLAME" someone else for "NOT" understanding you and your "PAIN"! "Sophia" knows it all too well! …trying to "BLAME" someone else for her "PAIN" instead of being "HONEST" and saying how "BAD" she was "HURT" and admitting her "Wrongs", even if it was "Pain" from what others have caused.

"Sophia" had no idea that it took more than her own strength. I know many have their own belief, and that's fine;

but when Sophia needed answers and more strength because her battles were too much and too "HEAVY" she knew she couldn't "TRUST" "NOBODY" but her belief of "PRAYING" to "GOD." She "NEVER" thought a person could cry so many tears.

She "NEVER" knew how much a person could cry until she had a "BREAKDOWN" in her "LIFE." There was "NOBODY" she could "TRUST" to talk about her personal situations. Only very few she allowed to let in to be close to her and all she needed was "PRAYER" at that point in her "LIFE." If you didn't have a "PRAYER" for Sophia you wasn't someone she needed to talk to in her "BROKEN" season.

"Women", this book wasn't just intended for you. "GOD" can do what He wants to do with the typing and the words that's "FLOWING" and the ways my fingers are moving. It's nothing like allowing "GOD" to have His way in your "LIFE", in all that you do, even concerning typing. "GOD" will always leads you the right way, His way, if you allow Him. "Ladies," you have to understand the "PAIN" isn't for you it's for another "WOMAN" that's "Dear" to you—even if it's a stranger or two.

"Sophia" had to "FORGIVE" many people, and she's still "HEALING." "MOST" people will say or ask why are you telling your business to people? "LOL," what business? My "PAIN" is other people's business, so people can see the "FINISHED" product of what "PAIN" looks like! When you can "HOLD" your head up ''HIGH" and keep a "SMILE" on your face, it says a lot about the person you really are on the inside. I know it's easier said than done but it's all worth it in the end. There's so much Sophia can share about what she has witnessed on what happens when you "FORGIVE" and "Pray"! I guess that's another story!

What I'm trying to say to the "Women" is, be more "KIND" to the "Women" who "God" sends to you, or even cross your path. Even if it's other "Women" outside of your family, no need to take things so personal. It's ok to "Fellowship" with other people. Sometimes it's easier to go outside of your comfort zone to experience something you've never had. You'll be '"AMAZED" at the people you will meet. Don't take any relationship for granted. If you allow yourself to be open to something different you'll begin to explore new people who are from different places, and they may even share a story or two with you; and don't be surprised if they share the exact same situations that you may be facing in the midst! "GOD" is "Funny" the way He does things!

10

Sometimes it takes us to do something we never done in order to get a different result.

Try "Praying"! It's a choice if you want to see things on the inside of you. You must stay there until you see a different result! Don't run! "HEALING" doesn't happen overnight—it's a process. It may sound strange, but it's truth. You may have to "Cry," "Cry," and "Cry" until there is no more tears on the inside of you. ...and even why you're crying those memories of pain that comes across your mind, that place right there, you ask God to "HEAL" you right there! Ask Him to take the pain away right their where you're "HURTING"! Stay in that "BREAKING" place. Listen to other people. "HUMBLE" yourself. You may even see yourself in them!

It's ok to be "Selfless" because "Life" isn't just about you. Are you tired of being the same person—the same way you were ten, fifteen years ago? ...the same conversations, the same negativity with no growth, and nothing still makes sense with the things you're still doing; and looking back at all those years you've wasted. A lot of times we're so busy looking at the next person and what they're doing and not paying attention to what's in our self. It's like we're grocery shopping so much in someone else's basket that we don't notice the eggs cracked in our basket!

11

"I know I know"! "Sophia" have to be "HONEST"—it's "REAL"! ...while you have your eyes on the other person "STRUGGLES", all you can do is "SPEAK" negative on that person? ...and no need to *expect* any positive words to hear, because "POSITIVITY" isn't on the inside of *you*! Remember, "HURT" people "HURT" people; so if people say you have done "Wrong" things towards them, it's only because they're "HURTING" on the inside, so no need to take it personally.

It's time to "LOVE" one another and get alone with one another. Sometimes it may even take someone to "EMBRACE" you to remind you it's going to be ok. It takes someone to be more "Compassionate" with you in order to allow you to open up; but first it starts with you setting the example before them on how to "LOVE" people. It doesn't necessarily mean giving over money to people. Many people think it's about money comforting you. Money can't buy you "LOVE" nor the "COMFORT" you're seeking. Money only makes "Life" easier.

It's ok to share your struggles and pain with others. It's ok to admit your flaws. It's ok to admit your "BROKENESS." Who cares what other's may think about you. Find another group of people where you can just be you, and be "Transparent"; and "Stand" up to those that you couldn't be yourself to. How do you know if it takes *you* to change in order for other people to see a difference on the inside of you? What if the new you wants to make them change something about *them*? How do you not know that "GOD" wants you to be the "LIGHT" for other people, in order to show them that through their "STRUGGLES" it's possible for a "NEW BEGINNING" for them!

It's for us to be the "LIGHT" for others, even when we're "BROKEN" on the inside. Your "PAIN" will produce a "Purpose" in your "LIFE" and those around you. There's no other way to bringing a change when *you're* not changing. What is your calling? Why? Don't you feel as if you're not "Meaningful" in someone else "LIFE"? What is it you want to do for others? What is your "HEART" desires? How would your "GOALS" and "DESIRES" help those "BROKEN" in your community? What are your motives? What is it that you want to see change? How are you working at you "Dreams" and bringing changes to those around you in your family?

It's ok to be "BROKEN." If you run into anyone that says they "NEVER" been "BROKEN," they're lying and it's "NO" "TRUTH" on the inside of them—even a "BLIND" man can see and feel pain. Let's not get "LIFE" twisted, even the "RICH" man go through things. Some people have no idea why their "LIFE" is filled with so much "HEARTACHE" and

"PAIN"; and they have no idea how to even release their pain. That's why so many people use "Smoking" and "Drinking" as a mechanism to "COPE" with the internal issues they're suffering in silence with; because they have no other way of dealing with the issues deep within.

We all have an way of "Coping" with "Pain", believe it or not, we all do. "Nobody" said "LIFE" will be easy but there are things we can do to make "LIFE" a little easier when we're not focused on our pain. It's ok to tell people the "TRUTH" on what you feel on the inside. It comes a time when you have to be "REAL" with you, and "Acknowledge" our issues we have—even if we can't seem to understand. It's time to get to the "ROOT" of the problem. If you know the reason why you're gay, and it started from childhood—admit to that. Many issues start from when we're a little child, and it festers into our adulthood, and our problems get worse. Save yourself from a lot of "HEATACHE" and "PAIN" and "ADDRESS" the issues. You "NEVER" know how your "BROKENESS" can be an "HEALING" to other people!

It's "Real"! There's too many people suffering in silence that need to hear your story; and "Never" be "ASHAMED" to admit where you're hurting and what caused you to hurt. People in the world may say mean things to you, but in "REALITY," the "GOD" "Sophia" serves, He's close to

the "BROKEN-HEARTED"! She knows that the "GOD" she
serves will bring "HEALING" in your heart, and gives
revelations in the midst of your pain! Things seem so bad
when you're going through; but when you begin to lay down
your "BURDENS" before "God" and tell him all about your
troubles, He already knows; but He's waiting on you to be
honest and talk to Him.

"Man," He'll give you answers to your questions, and
open your eyes to see why you had to endure. It'll make so
much sense as to why you even had to feel the pain you had to
feel. My "God," it's like a load that will be lifted up off you,
and you will feel a hundred pounds lighter! "God" will give
you the "PEACE" the world could "NEVER" give! I mean it's
such an "AMAZING" feeling just to lay in your "Father's"
arms. Whatever you want "God" to be to you, He's all that and
a bag of chips, plus some!

Well I want you all to remember that there is always
"BEAUTY" in your "BROKENESS." Keep on "Pressing,"
and keep on "Smiling," and know that someone out there is
depending on your strength. Who cares what the world says or
thinks about you? "TRUST "GOD" doesn't look at you the
way people in the world does, God thinks way differently of
you!!! "GOD" only knows who you "TRULY" are inside and

out; and He cares about your well-being, and He's not "Ashamed" to say you're His own! I'm telling y'all, try "GOD"! He "LOVES" you and your "BROKENESS," and He will wipe every tear that falls from your eyes!

CHAPTER 2

THE PLAN

What is the purpose of Women coming together? Is it to discredit one another? How can you say you "LOVE" someone, and your heart is filled with evil intentions? What is your purpose on earth as a "Woman"? Why is it that your "HEART" is so cruel towards every person you meet? Why do you find fault in other "Women" and try to rob them of their dignity in order to make yourself feel important?

Why is it that you "BEAT" the next "Black" Woman down with so much evil intent? Why are you so cruel, and so "HEARTLESS"? Why is it that us "BLACK" "Women" are so comfortable at calling the next "BLACK" "Woman" a "HOE," or a "BITCH"? Do you even know the real meaning of anyone of those names? Are you a female dog? Or better yet, are you a tool? ...then we wonder why "BLACK" Men call us

"BLACK" "Women" out of our names; because, we are who we answer to. When you begin to carry yourself as if you're a "Queen", expect to be treated like a "QUEEN." We want the "MEN" to treat us like a queen but we don't even carry ourselves like one.

Come on "Women", we have to do better than what we're doing. What is your purpose as a "WOMAN"? How is it that you say one thing but show another? What is your purpose of wanting to be a "Woman" of "Empowerment"? What is your purpose of "HURTING" other "WOMEN"? Is it to gain the social media attention in order for you to feel important? It's the "Wrong" attention you're drawing to yourself; and you still want someone to respect you for who you are? How do you treat yourself?

What type of "Woman" are you deep down on the inside? Who are *you?* ...ask yourself over and over again. Do you even understand your destiny and the gifts you carry within? How many people are you reaching in order to make a difference in their life? How effective are you? What's hurting you? Who scarred you? What was your upbringing like? Have you ever had to struggle? If so, how? Why bring your pain upon other people?

Everyone wants to ask the question why me; but, why not you? Do you know the "Power" you hold, in order to save many? What happened in your "Life" that was "Life" changing? Who were the people in your "LIFE" that told you that you weren't going to amount to anything? Who told you all those "HURTFUL" words and it "deteriorated" in your spirit—where you grew to be angry, bitter, and filled with so much hate. Nobody has to totally understand you; but many can relate to you!

Understand that it comes a time in your life where you have to forgive, forget, and live your life. It's ok to share your story, but how long will you stay down in that hurtful place? When would you dust your shoulders off and stand back up on your own two feet? You can't depend on nothing or nobody in this world to get anything for you—not even your healing. You have to want it! *You* have to be the one that wants a change! *You* have to encourage yourself to be better than what you are! It doesn't matter what you've gone through—it's about how far you see yourself going, and how far you're going to go.

Everyone won't be happy for you if you decide to change and leave them behind in order to make yourself a better you. It hurts when you have to leave those you love behind you in order to protect you. It hurts more when you have to walk away from those you "LOVE" in order to find yourself and "Healing." You have to try! You have to keep pushing! You have to keep pressing! You have to keep pushing! Don't you "DARE" give up and give in now! You're almost there! You're almost there at the "BREAKING" point in your "LIFE." You have to give in, you can't give up!

…so what if they talked about you? …so what if they walked away? So what if they stole from you? So what if they left you for dead? …so what if your "HURTING" right now? …so what if your heart is "BLEEDING"? …so what if you want to cry and punch a hole in a wall! Don't you "DARE" give up; keep striving! …so what if you have to start from scratch! …so what if you have to be down a season? …so what if you lost everything you've ever had? Keep on pushing…! Your past doesn't define who you are! Your past should help you even the more to become the person you want to be in your future!

"STOP" telling yourself you're too old, or you're no good—it's too many people in the world that needs someone like you to help them. "STOP" believing the lies of what the people said about you. Shake it off and keep on pushing—you are the "LIFE LINE" in someone's life. You know the "Good *and* Bad" that's held on the inside of you! You know that idea that keeps popping up in your head on what you should do! …that vision that keeps popping up in your mind about what your heart feels on what you should be doing! Don't let anything hold you back! "No Pain" should be able to stop you from making your dreams comes true!

You are responsible for you. Don't "BLAME" nobody but yourself when you're not being successful! If you think about some of the most popular celebrities and where they came from, and where they're at today, they have a story just as well—like you. *Now* what's your excuse of not reaching your destiny? You have to keep pressing towards the mountain until you get there. Even if you have to set goals for yourself and cross them out as you go, do so. Life doesn't stop because of "PAIN". We all have pain, we all go through something— you're not alone. Your "PURPOSE" is to "Defeat" every "GIANT" that you've had to face, and move it out your way, and keep pressing towards the mountain.

Everything you've ever encountered in your "LIFE" has an good or bad ending; but does it mean that you quit? No! Your purpose is to win, and let nothing hold you back from winning. It doesn't matter how old you are, get there—achieve your goals! Your purpose is to do what your heart desires to do in order to share with other people what it took for you to get where you are today. Be "Honest" about the "HELL" you've been through! Even when you're hurting, who cares if it was nobody but you that went through your storm alone.

No need to "BLAME" other people for what you're not putting time into. Allow your focus to be on what it's supposed to be on, and that's what's in front of you, not behind you—not looking into the rear view mirror. Keep looking forward because if you keep looking back in your rear-view mirror, your future will always look bleak. Your purpose is to be determined to keep pressing forward, and keep pushing towards the mountains. Failure is "NOBODY" else fault but your own, not the people that scarred you. Nobody could be the person you we're called to be but you.

So what are you going to do about it? What is that very one thing you want to do? Did you try? Have you started somewhere with your vision on that dream? What's holding you back from your purpose? Who are you "BLAMING" for your "Failure"? How is it that you hold the "KEY" to your destiny and you allow someone else to take the "POWER" you hold on the inside of you away—as if they control you and your life decisions? Other people only have the "POWER" over your "LIFE" when you *give* them the "POWER" in your "LIFE."

…so why do you allow the enemy to have the "Power and Control" over your "LIFE"? Don't be "Fooled" by the kind words from people that will knock you out of your square! Stay focused in your own lane, and keep your eyes on your vision! You will be better than you've been before.

People think their own "LIFE" is just about them, but it's "NOT"! What about those around you that's "HURTING" and "WOUNDED"? There's no way you should "ENJOY" seeing those around you in "PAIN". Some witness other people's pain and "STRUGGLES," and still "Overlook" them—as if they're "NOT" a human-being. Come on body of "CHRIST", we have to do better than what we're doing! But, we all should know "Hurt people Hurt people", and it's no other way around it! Your "PURPOSE" should be to build one another up in this world today!

You never know who you may be a "BLESSING" to. You "NEVER" know who you "MAY" be connected to. The same ones you're "LAUGHING" at today can become "MILLIONARES" tomorrow! They "MAY" be the same ones that may want to "BLESS" you but walk right past you. How do you "NOT" know your "Purpose" may be to help someone in need to reserve a hard time in your "FUTURE" "Life"? What if that same person that's been "Weighing" on your "HEART" may be a "Spiritual connection" for you to help them, that may be reserved to help your children one day?

How do you not know that "HELPING" others will become "HEALING" for your "LIFE" and "Pain"? How far does being "SELFISH" take you?

How could you be so "HEARTLESS", when there's so many "HURTING" people in this cold world? How can you walk pass someone that's hungry and they ask you for a dollar, and you have a pocket full of money, and you go home to a warm home. How much will you give when your "FAITH" is being "TESTED"? How can you "HOLD" back from those you can make a difference to—even if they're a complete stranger? What were you born to do? …to work all your "LIFE" and withhold everything you ever *owned*?

How are you reaping from not sowing? Do you really believe that with your fist being balled-up you'll experience the "Overflow" of "Blessings"? What will you do when your "Job" isn't making you happy? What will you do if your bank account "FREEZES"? What will you do if everything you worked so "HARD" for is gone or taken away from you? What if someone took everything away from you—robbed you from everything you've ever owned? What kind of seed did you plant in the "LIVES" of people? What are you teaching your children—to make "Broken Promises" to you? What world are you "Living" in where you're ok as long as you have everything you need that you hold on to dearly.

24

Sophia Long

I guess "NOBODY" else mean a "DAM" thing to you! It's all good, "Sophia" hear many stories of why people shouldn't "Bless" others, or be a "Blessing." She still "NEVER" understood such things of many people. …"EXCUSES" of why they shouldn't be a "Blessing" to those in need. "Sophia" has heard many stories: "I'm "NOT" giving that "MAN" no "Money," he better go get a "JOB," (even though he's on the streets, looking not so clean) but have no idea of that "MAN" story behind his situation!

"You "STUPID" for helping that family of "FIVE," when you "Sophia" have "Five" children of your own! …the mean things, "Sophia" couldn't understand about people. …too bad "SOPHIA'S" heart isn't so cruel! She's glad she's "NOT" like other people! She's "HAPPY" she experienced situations of the people she witnesses on the streets. "Sophia" can relate on different levels, with many people situations. "Sophia" always had a "BIG" heart to "GIVE," even if it was the "WRONG" people with "ALTERIOR" motives.

"Nobody" could ever change that about "Sophia" unless she was fed up of someone misusing her—that's when she knew her time was up with them. "Sophia" sure wasn't a "FOOL", even with her having a "BIG HEART! She knows

25

all those that have used her for their own reasoning. "Sophia" began to look at situations in a "Totally" different perspective. "Sophia" knew that her "PURPOSE" was to help people—even if it meant them taking "NOTES" from her all in the end. Some people "NEVER" even said "THANK YOU", but it's ok! "Most" people needed "Sophia" more than she needed them! That's "FACTS"! If you wasn't "Forty and over" it was "Nothing" you could really teach "Sophia."

"Sophia" knows her "Purpose"! She knows she was called to "HELP" many people: "Homeless people," those in "Prison," "Shelters," those around her, "Battered Women," "Single Mothers," "Children," "Youth," "Drug Dealers," and so much more—only because she has been in those places or either experienced those places, or could have ended up in some situations—without a doubt. "Sophia" understands that her "Purpose" of "LIVING" her "Life" isn't her own! Despite of "Sophia" having five children, she still strives to "Help" others in need—even when having financial difficulties! "Sophia" doesn't like to see many suffering if she's able to help the situation.

"Sophia" doesn't understand herself at times, why she even do the things she does. Sometimes she gets tired and wants to give up. ...times she wants to throw in the "Towel," but she knows she have to keep "Pressing" and "Pushing" because of knowing her children needing her. "Sophia" has always asked herself do anyone sees *her*? "Yes", "Sophia" feels invisible *many* times! It's times she feels as she's an "Invisible Angel" walking on earth. There's times she don't understand how she's even *surviving* the "LIFE" she has! "Sophia" doesn't understand why she was *placed* on "Earth" at times, because of so much "PRESSURE" and demonic attacks she has been under. ...but, she does know "God" is "Real"! "Sophia" wants to remind you that her belief may not be your belief. "NO PRESSURE"!

The more you go through in "LIFE" you should notice what your "Purpose" is, especially when "Life" keeps taking you around and around in circles. Have you ever thought about why have you been going through the same things over and over again? "Why" Hasn't anything changed? "Hmmm," is it you? "What" are you doing differently? What have you been exercising in order to change you, or your bad habits? Do you enjoy the things you "Tolerate" in your *own* "LIFE"? What "JOY" do you get out of the things you do? How are you bringing about change again? Are you "Walking the Walk," and "Talking the Talk" with the things you're doing, in order to change? How many years have you allowed time to pass you by? Did you make any effort to "PUSH" towards your "DESTINY"?

You've been saying you we're going back to school the last seven years, did you? Or did you allow another seven years to pass you by? You want to feed the "Homeless," did you? How "Hard" is it to put your "FEET" in front of the other? How long will you "DWELL" in that "Low self-esteem", and "Lack of Confidence"? I'm talking about "Sophia" as well? How many "EXCUSES" do we have to make up for *us* being "STAGNANT"?

Who do you think is effected by your "PURPOSE" in "LIFE"? Who do you think you're effecting by "NOT" pursuing your purpose? You're only "HURTING" you, and "NOBODY" else! Are you tired of "BLAMING" other people? Are tired yet? "Let's" be "REAL", who are you "Competing" with? Who are you to "COMPETE" with, and you don't even know how to follow simple instructions! "Come-on" now, this isn't "BABY" talk, it's "ADULT-PROVISION."

Let's be "REALISTIC", and be "REAL", and "HONEST" with ourself concerning "LIFE" situations! When you're "MATURE" enough to handle "BOLDNESS" you would be able to handle "ADULT" conversations without "RUNNING" or "GROUPING UP"—as if you need someone to hold your hand and needing someone to wear your own "BIG-GIRL" panties, or needing someone to put their feet inside of your shoes, when "CLEARLY" the shoes don't even fit!

It doesn't gets any "REALER" with "SOPHIA" and the things she say, but it's "TRUTH". She understands "MOST" people can't "HANDLE" the "TRUTH"! That's why she doesn't have "FRIENDS" now. "LOL", because "Sophia" is going to "ALWAYS" tell people the "TRUTH" whether they like her or not! "Sophia" don't have time to tell "NOBODY" what they want to "HEAR" because she doesn't want no "YES" people around her! "Sophia" don't have room for the "NON-SENSE" and if she have to be "LESS" than who she is for anyone, that means she needs to separate herself and find those that's "MATURE" enough to handle the person she is!

"Sophia" don't gives "TWO-FUCKS" about those that don't like her, don't speak or call her. She's ok in her own space, keeping her "PEACE", and staying away from the "FAKE & PHONY." She has "NO ROOM" for any "NON-SENSE" or "FAKENESS" because she knows who she is! "Sophia" knows her "Purpose". She knows the important things she has to do in her "LIFE" that's "VALUABLE", and the things that's "NOT VALUABLE"! She will choose the

"VALUABLE" things in "LIFE" more than her "UNDER-VALUING" herself! Just as well as "Sophia" knows who she is, she advise other people to get to know who they are, and know their value in "LIFE", in the things they need to do.

"Sophia" encourages everyone to take a moment in their "LIFE" and take a look at themselves in the mirror and take a good look, and think about what they would, should, and could of change in order for them to be a better person. "Sophia" wants everyone she knows to be better than what they are, and she would "HOPE" others feel the same way about her as well! We all were born into a "SINFUL" world, but are you going to remain to be a "SINFUL" person in this "SINFUL" world? Or are you going to take action and do things differently?

Those that "Walk in this "WORLD" alone, "Please" don't think that you're alone; and people are afraid to take a "STAND" to those that tries to put "FEAR" on the inside of you. You look at that situation, and you tell that situation to get under your feet! It's ok to start off your "Purpose" just wanting to travel, well make plans and just go! Pack your bags and go! "Sophia" knows how hard it can be in order to "BREAK" the "BAD" habits in your "LIFE"; but even when under "PRESSURE" you have to keep the "FIGHT" on the inside of you! "NEVER" give up because you're a

"WINNER"! Who cares if "NOBODY" ever tells you they're "PROUD" of you—you better keep going, and "DON'T" "STOP" what you're doing!

So *what* if you have to go "TREAT" yourself to dinner, buy yourself "FLOWERS"? Who cares if "NO-ONE" hugs you, "HUG" yourself! Who *cares*? "SOPHIA" has to do it, and so can you! Take time out just for *you*. "LOVE" *you,* and figure out what you want for you, because "NOBODY" else will! Remember you can't enjoy "FREEDOM" unless you've been "BOUND"; so "SHAKE" yourself loose and keep moving your feet!

It's no excuses and "NO LIMIT" to the things *you* can do! You can do all things through "CHRIST" Who "STRENGTHENS" you! You're "NOT" alone! It's someone out here going through just like you—if not worse. Always keep that in mind. "Keep Reaching" towards your "VISIONS," keep "PRESSING" towards the "STARS"! You got this "JOURNEY" called "LIFE." Ask yourself what "LEGACY" will you leave behind? Let no-one tell you, "You can't". When they say you can't, tell yourself "you can"!

Be "TRUE" to your "PURPOSE", and keep setting goals for yourself, and keep achieving—even if you have to try over, and over again. Keep climbing until you reach your

"DESTINY"! Only you can grab your "DESTINY" and "STAND" on your own two feet! "KEEP REACHING"!

CHAPTER 3

THE PURPOSE

What is your plan and the goals you want to accomplish? How did you know your childhood hurt and scar wasn't for your good? How do you not know that your absent "Father" not being there was for your good and protection? How do you not know that your "Drug addict" "Mother" was to bring out the best in you? How do you not know that the "Molestation" was a part of sharing and caring for other people?

How do you not know that raising your children alone would bring out the "BEST" in you? How do you "Not" know that your "Adoption" was for you to adopt children later in your own "Life?" How do you "NOT" know if that child you once "Miscarried" was to have "LOVE" for other children?

How do you not know if being in the "Foster care system" allowed you to be an example to other children?

How do you "NOT" know that the "Struggle" you're in today, is going to be a "BETTER" outcome for your tomorrow? "How" do you "NOT" know that that abusive relationship you were once in makes you have "Compassion" for other victims? How do you not understand it's all a part of "GOD" plan for your "LIFE"? No, it's not about being religious when speaking the truth, its life that has already been written on things you go through. How do you get out? How do you walk away? How do you "TRULY" Forgive" when people in "LIFE" have "BEAT" you down.

Some people have been "MISLEAD" to show their "EGO" versus their "WEAK" side. Some people would call it being "TOUGH." How do you survive when it seems as if "NOBODY" is on your side? When you're feeling alone and you have no idea what's in store for your "LIFE." There's been so many "DARK" clouds, and "Dark" moments, and situations that have occurred in your "LIFE." It can be hard to think positive when your facing so many "DRAMATIC" changes in your "LIFE".

Many people "NEVER" had people to "FEND" for them, and they were left alone to fight for everything they've ever owned. How can you see the "Purpose" and "Plan" for your "Life" with so many "BLIND" spots that has happened in your "LIFE"? What is a person to think when all "HELL" is "BREAKING" loose, and "Nobody" is there to take up for you? Then when you walk in silence and don't want to share a tear or neither wanting to be "Confrontational," people will think you're "STUPID" or "Slow," or either have some type of "Mental" illness when you don't respond to the "Negativity" people bring. Many times "Sophia" had to ask "GOD" why, but then his response was: "WHY" not you?

Many nights alone, walking through "Dark" moments pretending like everything was ok, with a "FAKE" smile we have to put on, so "NOBODY" can sense any "WEAK" side or "PAIN" you're feeling on the inside; but in silence, your "HEART" is "BROKEN," "Hoping" and "Wishing" nobody smells your "Fear" of having to keep your head up in the midst of your "PAIN." You're not even understanding what's happening on the inside of you—which is "NOTHING" but "GROWING" pain growing on the inside of you. What are you thinking? What is the "PLAN" for my "LIFE"? Will I always "STRUGGLE"? Whose "DEFENDING" your name when the whole world seems to be against you, and you have to continue to "Fight" and argue to make people understand who the "FUCK" you are.

35

The Purpose

What is the "PLAN" for my "LIFE" with all the "DRAMA" I'm dealing with? ...soo many "FAKE" and "PHONY" people! ...knowing "DEEP" down on the inside that "SHIT" isn't you! Who is "DEFENDING" you or your name? You're so sick and tired of running the streets, trying to make ends meet. Not sure which way to go and so many people to see; but "NOBODY" "TRULY" understands what even makes you weak.

So many people have so many "EXCUSES" taking on the duties in their busy "Lives" they "FORGET" about you and your situation in the streets. ...still wondering what "GOD" have in "PLAN" for your "LIFE." Many people are busy thinking it's in the "MEN," "NIGGAS," and the "HOES," and "BITCHES" in the streets, when secretly we all have our own personal "AGENDAS" in order to get through "LIFE." ...still wondering what "PLAN" does "GOD" have for me? Seems that if it can't be "LOVE," it can't be "LIFE" when "LIFE" have scorn you into little bitty pieces. Hoping and wishing, not wanting to wake up in the early morning because of the "BULLSHIT" that's going on around you—and "NOTHING" seems to catch you by surprise!

Even those that say they do and don't believe in "GOD" will even ask the questions "WHY"? "WHY" so much "PAIN" if "GOD" is "REAL"? How do you not know if it's

"GOD" allowing "BAD" things to happen in your "LIFE" in order to get your attention, in order to give you understanding and "REVELATION" in your "LIFE", in order to show you what He has in store for you?

"Nobody" really wants to listen to what anyone have to say about "GOD"! Many people aren't trying to listen to what "GOD" uses people to say! Everyone wants to "LEAN" towards their own understanding and ideas, as to why they're going through the "HELL" they're going through; but whose watching over you? Whose telling you the "TRUTH" about what's going on with you in your "LIFE?" How many people have "STRIVED" to help you see "LIFE" differently? "How" long will you keep lying to yourself and keep allowing yourself to see "LIFE" they same since your childhood? "Where" did you allow yourself to grow to be open to be new teaching in order to understand the "PURPOSE" in your "LIFE"? How do you not know if "GOD" has sent an "ANGEL" to speak to you in a "HUMAN" form, and you just wasn't used to that type of "LANGUAGE" because you didn't understand what they were saying.

Many people miss their opportunity when your seeking for answers and you missed the answer to your "PRAYERS". I know we all may have ran into someone that has crossed our path in the midst of us "HURTING", and said some "POSTIVE" words that has stick with you until this day. "Sophia" can witness that running into people throughout her "LIFE" when she would complain and someone would say something positive to help encourage her until this day. She still thinks about a lot of people that has spoken into her "LIFE" when she needed it the "MOST"! What a "BLESSING" in "DISGUISE" for "Sophia", especially as you get older and think about the people that crossed your path, and it still has it's meaning down through the years. That says a lot—that those type of people were "HEAVENLY" people that meant well.

It's a reason why we go through what we go through. It's ok to feel as if you don't know what's going on, or asking yourself questions about what your plan in your "LIFE" is. It's not the time to "Procrastinate" and be "STAGNANT", it's time to write down your plan and go for what it is that you want to do. "STOP" looking for other people to do things for you. You have to do what needs to be done for yourself; and do one step at a time. Once you encourage yourself and tell yourself you can do it, you can do it! Get the negative words out of your mind. Don't allow yourself to set your mind on the negative thoughts and things in this world that distract you from the plans God set for your "LIFE."

Everyone isn't going to be happy for you, so it's better to keep silent and do what it is you have to do. It's ok if "NOBODY" supports you. Remember, what don't "KILL" you will only make you "STRONGER"! You have to be the one to "Pursue" on what you have to get done, instead of focusing on what other's think of you! Nobody but *you* can determine your "DESTINY" and your outlook in "Life." Your "PLAN" is your "PLAN"; and if you allow other people to rob you from your "PLAN", it's your own fault and nobody else's fault.

There's a lot of people that come up with many excuses on why they didn't "PURSUE" their dreams; and "NO," there's no "JUDGING" because "Sophia" wish she would have did a few things in her "LIFE" when she was younger; and her only excuse was she didn't want to leave her baby behind. As he was a toddler just learning how to walk and busy licking a chicken-bone, he was busy enjoying his first steps and eating some mashed potatoes. "Lil Ron-Ron" wasn't thinking about his "Mother" Sophia! Whose going to be the one to "STOP" making excuses for themselves and do what their "HEART" is yearning to do? "NOBODY" will understand the "JOURNEY" "GOD" has you on but you and Him is what "SOPHIA" would say to you!

There were many people that has "PROMISED" "Sophia" many things for many years; and if she was to hear someone tell her a "PROMISE" today it would "HONESTLY" go in one ear and out the other very quickly. She hopes they mean well, and be either a "MAN" or "WOMAN" of their word; but, "Sophia" so used to so many "FAKE and Phony" people that she discerns a "LIE" and she knows when someone is "LYING" to her! "Sophia" has heard so many lies from those she "TRUSTED" or "CONFIDED" in as a little girl, and just about every person she ever knew have done more "HARM" than being "TRUTHFUL"! "Come-on" now, do you really think "SOPHIA" believe just anything you tell her? What "WORLD" are y'all living in? How do you not know that the story that "Sophia" is sharing with you is because of her personal experiences?

Do you know how many people have "BROKEN" "Sophia" "Spirit down," "Backstabbed," "Betrayed," "left her for Dead," "Mislead," "Lied," "Cheated," "Broke Promises," "Laughed," "Mocked," "Discredited" her name? People have even talked about her and her children, and promise her and her children many things. But "Sophia" realized that she couldn't put her "TRUST" in anyone because people are "FLESH." She learned that a lot of people like to say things in order to make them feel important and pretend to be something they're

"NOT"! Which has been "GREAT" motivation for "Sophia" to stick with her own "VISION" and "PLAN", and stay in her own lane.

"Sophia" has always looked at every situation and lesson she has gone through with other people, and "Meditated" on the "Good" out of the "NEGATIVE"—even if it caused her pain! Not many people have been there for "SOPHIA" in a "PURE" way; it was always to "GAIN" for their own selfish reasons! It's crazy how so many people have plans and won't share with you the "Tools and Knowledge" that it took to get there. So many people that say they want you to "SUCCEED" are sometimes the main ones who "Secretly" expect you to "FAIL." Some people are afraid of sharing their ideas, and have the "Provision" for your "LIFE" and still wouldn't share their thoughts with you! If some people decide to share, they think they now can control you based on the ideas they've shared with you.

There's so many "SNAKES" that stay "HISSING" around you, waiting on the right moment to "BITE" you. "TRUST", "Sophia" knows it all too well with those wanting to be close, and nothing you're learning from them; but come to you as if you're their research guide. People will come around you just to try to steal your ideas and your "PLANS"

41

for your "LIFE", as if they were someone that will stick by you, thinking they're on the same page and lane with you, just to find out they were "NOTHING" but a "DISTRACTION" to hinder you. "LIFE" has to get "BETTER" to those that's seeking "BETTER"…and only those that are "WILLING", and "OBEDIENT", and who can follow instructions for the directions in their "LIFE."

No matter how much people have "Doubted you and Discouraged" you better stick to the "PLAN" and "Visions" that has been set before you. It's ok to share your ideas! If you feel in your heart anyone you go to, and they don't seem to have the right answers to your questions—you keep seeking, you keep pressing. Even when you're asking for information, and you begin to feel deep down in your gut that they're lying to you—you keep a smile on your face, and don't allow them to see you sweat. It doesn't matter how bad they may hurt your feelings, it doesn't mean you throw in the towel because of them.

You better "NOT" "DARE" give up and take a "NO" for an answer! I don't care if you have to go through ten people and it's all a "NO", you "BETTER" "NOT" give in! Keep going until you get what you're seeking. That's a lot of people problem—how we give up too easily, just because things don't go as we "PLAN." That doesn't mean that the way we see or think certain things should go the way we see them, that your "VISION" is in "VAIN".

How do you not know if your "REJECTION" is part of your "HEALING"? How do you not know if your "HEALING" is in your "REJECTION"? How do you "NOT" know if your "DESPERATION" and "WILLINGNESS" of "NOT" giving in will open up doors more than you could ever "Imagine"? What if you had to be connected to the "Wrong" people in order to connect with the "RIGHT" people that want to see you "WIN"—all because you "NEVER" threw in the towel? How do you know you're "NOT" feeling the "PRESSURE" because you're about to catch the "BIGGEST" "BREAK" in your "LIFE"?

"LET the "PAIN" Go", "Let the Agony Go"— "SOPHIA" is even encouraging herself. There's no way you could have told her she was going to be an inspiration to others. There's no way you was going to tell "Sophia" her "LIFE" would be changing for the "BETTER"! She might have looked at you like you were crazy! You couldn't tell "Sophia" that she was going to get through the "HELL" she has been through. I even "DARE" you to even tell her that she was even going to "OVERCOME" every obstacles in her "LIFE" with her "LIFE" that's been filled with nothing but

"PAIN." You couldn't tell Sophia" she was going to even "WIN" and have the "V-I-C-T-O-R-Y" all in the end! The devil used so many people to try and "BREAK" "Sophia" into many pieces; how "Dare" you to even *think* she was going to make it through the "HELL" she's gone through.

There's no way a "Human-being" should have been through so much in "LIFE" at so young, and still "WELL-ALIVE" and still "BREATHING." "Sophia" should have been "MENTALLY RETARED," if not that then somewhere in a "MENTAL INSTUITUTION," or "SIX FEET" under! "Sophia" sure thought her "LIFE," "DREAMS," and "PLANS" were over. The thought of her having children, five on top of that, and raising them alone—not even a "MAN'S" vows can change anything if his "HEART" isn't "PURELY" into making a change and putting "FAMILY" first. "Sophia" sure tries to share with so many "YOUNG" people that just because you have a baby by a "MAN" doesn't means he will stay. I mean it's "NOTHING" like being "HONEST" and telling the next generation the "TRUTH," "HOPING" they avoid the pattern you've taken in your "LIFE."

I mean there's so many, I mean *many* people in the "WORLD" today "HURTING" from something they've "NEVER" let go of; and many of us have brought the "PAIN" into our "ADULT" "LIFE". It's sad, more so

44

"HEARTBREAKING" when you sit back and pay attention to everything that is happening. People are in "PAIN," seeking for "HEALING," and have no idea of the people or place to turn to; so they "HARBOR" their "PAIN" on the inside. I mean look at the "WAR" that's going on the outside physically, just imagine the "WAR" that's "RAGING" on the inside of a "Human Being."

How do you not know people act out of "ANGER" and cuss you out because they really don't know how to "EXPRESS" how they feel on the inside to you? If you think about why "ABUSERS" abuse other people, do you think they want to? Or is it because they may have "Anger" issues? "Nobody" will ever get to the "REAL" root of their problems until they're able to look at their self in the mirror. Why do you think "MEN" cheat? Could it be that it's something they were taught to do, or is it because there was "NEVER" any "REAL" male role models that was "POSITIVE" in their "LIFE"? "Why" do you think there are so many "TEENAGERS" having babies? Could it be there was "NO" "Father" at home? Or could it be that child felt "Abandoned," being in a "Foster" home, going from place to place...and that "TEEN" "Mother" felt that she just wanted someone to "LOVE"?

It doesn't matter what type of "PAIN" you're in, don't ever get distracted from you "PLAN". It's ok to take some time out to "HEAL". We all have to take a moment and "'Breathe" in order to "PUSH" past your "PAIN." "Sophia" has felt many times (even now in the midst of her writing her story) "Discouraged"; but she still knows that her "Honesty" and "Pressing" will be a "HEALING" to others for their "LIFE." She wants everyone to succeed, and "THRIVE" to everything they set their mind to, because she knows if she could do it anybody can. If "Sophia" didn't find an "EXCUSE" to "GIVE UP", why should you.

She has had many reason to throw in the "TOWEL." Do you know how "HARD" it has been to keep her head over "WATER" and not "COMMIT SUICIDE"? Do you really understand that it couldn't have been "SOPHIA'S" only "STRENGTH"? Do you not know if it was up to "SOPHIA", she would have "BLEW" her own "BRAINS" out?

So once again, she's reminding you, if you want to go back to school, start somewhere. Research schools and enroll, go do it! If you want to design, sign up for a class and go! If you want to be a hairstylist, do it! Remember, "Sophia" didn't have too many people to encourage her to do anything "POSTIVE"; but she now have the opportunity to reach other people to do what others should have done to her when she was fourteen in the streets, hanging with older "WOMEN" that just wanted to hand her a "DRINK and a BLUNT". "FUCK" school! That's the type of "SHIT" "Sophia" was introduced to; but it's ok—those older 'WOMEN' were "HURTING" to.

How could anyone be a "GUIDE" of "GUIDANCE" unto you when their "HURTING" just as well as you? Only a "REAL" "Woman" is going to tell the next "Young" "Woman" the "TRUTH" about what's really going on in this world today and "POUR" "Wisdom" on the inside of them. It's "NOT" about the "Smoking," "Drinking," "Partying," "NIGGAS," or the "Strip clubs"; and neither the "HOES" and "Bitches" either. "Sophia" is just keeping it "REAL" and giving it "Raw and Uncut" on how the world "Misperceives" it, as if that's what it's about. "Sophia" been there and done that, and been down that road as well; and "NOTHING" will take place on her watch if she can help any situation. If "Sophia" was to be spotted in those situations, please "TRUST" it's all for the right reasons…and a lot of times, it's "NONE" of your "BUSINESS"! It's between "Sophia" and "GOD" business!

"LOL," anyhow, make part of your "PLAN" to "HEAL." Allow your "HEALING" to be effective where you begin to see things differently, and most of all clearly. "Nobody" has to understand you and the things you do or what you do in secret; and those who's "Reading," I "HOPE" you're "Listening"! Take notes and take "HEED," because "MOST" people will say "Sophia" is sharing too much information! Who cares...that's the "DIFFERENCE"...you're "NOT" "Sophia"! She has to be "HONEST" because "NOT" many people know what being "HONEST" really means! So gone on, sit back, and let your "HEALING" journey begin—it starts with you.

CHAPTER 4

THE HEALING

How does "HEALING" even begin when you've been "Damaged," and "BEAT" down to the core, and it seems that as you finished "HEALING" from one situation then here comes another bump in the road? How do you pick up the pieces? When will the "Healing" begin? "Sophia" knows it's hard when you think about all the troubles you've been through and it seems as your past tries to come right back in your future to "Discourage" you. "Nobody" seems to have an explanation for your situations and the darts that's been thrown at you.

There's no way it seems like you'll be able to heal when darts have been sent to destroy you on every level. How can you tell someone that their "LIFE" and situations will get better if their heart has been "BROKEN" into millions of pieces? How can you "DARE" encourage someone that "LIFE" will get better for them when they're in such a "Dark"

49

place in their "LIFE" and "Healing" seems like it never even begins, as if every feeling is left the same and nothing seems to change. It's just been too much pain, too much blood shed in the hearts. "How" do you keep surviving when your heart is "Heavy" and the "Burdens" are heavy to the point where it becomes baggage?

How do you "Heal" when you think about the pain in your "childhood" and still is in recovery? How do you "Heal" when you've been a "victim" of "molestation" and it was caused by those you loved and once "Trusted"? What is "Forgiveness"? What if every time you've tried to climb up the "mountain" you found yourself falling right back down? "Sophia" knows how it feels when you take ten steps forward, and it seems as if you get knocked down five steps backwards.

How can you encourage someone that their dark season is only temporary? How can you get others to believe you, and get them to understand you have been in the same shoes they're in—which in all honesty, it's up to you in order to believe, to witness the miracle, and have the "Confidence" in order to receive the "Breakthrough" in your "Life". Don't "waiver", just "Trust" that one day you're going to come out of the situation you're in. Everything you've ever endure is only a "Test" of your "Faith", which it's the "Truth". You're not alone in the "Battles" and unanswered questions of why you're with so much pain.

"Nobody" knew what they were going to experience in "LIFE". No one warned us about what we were going to face from a "Newborn", to a "Toddler", "Teenager", to our adulthood. "Nobody" was prepared on what "Life" would have had in store for them. Of course, nobody asked to be here; but it's a "Blessing" that your still "living and breathing", even though it's been much "grief" in our "Lives".

How do you not know that the "Pain" in your feeling is "Healing" for someone else? Your "Healing" is "Healing" for someone else "Deliverance", your "Healing" is someone else "Happiness", Your "Healing" is someone else "Restoration", "Lifeline"... How do you not know if your "Healing" is someone else "Breakthrough" for their next promotion— because in the midst of your process of "Healing" your someone else "Eye-opener" in order for them to see something different.

"No" need to "Discredit" your name and doubt the person you are in order to make someone else feel better. You are someone else "Light" in a "Dark" place. "Sophia" would say "God" sees and He knows all about the things you're going through. It's no secret, what's been "Hurting" you nor weighing heavy on you. There's no need to carry dead-weight on you if you can make a difference in your situation. There's no way you should feel bad about the situation or pressure you're feeling.

Some people may ask how can you received your "HEALING"? "How" do you begin to "Heal" with your pain? It may take you to have some time out for just yourself, and find a quiet and secret place where you can only hear you and no noise, even if it takes you to be alone in this journey. So what if you have to disconnect yourself from everyone and be alone, or it may even take you to turn off your phone and have no type of distractions around or near you.

There's no way you should not be able to make time for yourself in order to find your "Healing" and face the things that has been "Hurting" you deep down on the inside. There's no reason to worry about what the other people may think about you. Who cares if people think you're acting funny for distancing yourself. You have to find the secret place within yourself in order to receive the "Proper Healing" that you need.

Some people may need years to "Heal," and you owe no one any explanation to what it is you're trying to do. Sometimes it may even take you to have "Faith" (as what "Sophia" will call it) to move out of your comfort zone and move to another state in order to find the "Real" you. No longer should you have any excuse on how you don't have any more or you have no idea where to begin, when "CLEARLY" "Sophia" is sharing the "Wisdom" on how she moved using her "Faith."

"Sophia" understands that some people may even say, well what works for you may not work for me. "Well," could it be that she's sharing so much because she knows that there is "Strength" and "Power" that you carry on the inside of you, and she's wanting you to see it. Look in the mirror and ask yourself who are you? "What" potentials do you carry? "How" can you speak more on "Evil'" than "Good" over your own "Life"? How can you allow someone to determine what you're not, and accept the "Evil" words they have spoken over your "Life"?

"How" dare you allow other people to "Drag" your name in the mud, and you take every "BLOW" and "SHED" tears. "How" dare you to receive the words of someone else's "Pain" and their "Evil" words they spoke of you because of the "Pain" they're feeling on the inside of them—and you not noticed there words was used to "Break" you down. There words are all they have in order to make them feel good on the inside and their heart as "bleeding" worser than yours on the inside and you allowed them to see you "Sweat". Always keep in mind, "Hurt" people, "Hurt" people. Those that always have something "Negative" to say or better yet those that like to sit up and "Gossip" about you or other people—pay attention to their character. If you're around other people and y'all sit around and "Gossip" about each other and y'all around the same types of people—"Guess" what, the same person you're "Gossiping" with is the same person sitting around the same people y'all just got finished talking about. He or she is now talking about you.

"Sophia" is just sharing the "Realities" of what happens in the "Streets," "Families," "Fake Friends," and even behind the scene in the "Church buildings," on your jobs, (let's be "Honest") and if you look at it like that, there's no way you can really think those around you isn't "Hurting" as well—maybe even "Worser" than you, and "Walking" around with "Fake" smiles. It sure wasn't just "Sophia" pretending to be "Happy"; and she was "Unhappy," "Beat-down," and "Broken" on the inside. It's time out for pretending to be "Happy" or coming up with excuses, as if people only "Hurt" you because you've done something to them. "No" that's "Not" how that works!

People attack you because secretly, they see something different on the inside of you. They can't seem to "Express" their self with "Truth" and just say what they really feel towards you—such as: "You're Beautiful," "You're

Handsome," "You look good today," "You have such a "Pretty" smile," "I'm Hurting,". but instead, they try to find ways to "Hurt" you in order to protect their "True" feelings on the inside. Whatever your feelings are on the inside, they will always come out of you one way or another.

"How" do you recognize when someone is "Hurting"? You will notice the "Behavior" in their attitudes, they would act out in "Aggression" that means there's a "Root" of "Hurt" that's in them. Who knows what it could be from? A childhood scar, a "Broken" heart from a "past relationship", a sense of "Loneliness", an "Abusive relationship", or even an absent parent not being at home. It can be various of reasons why someone can act out the way they do; and it's not just the children, its adults as well.

Many people that have issues are ashamed to seek any treatment, as if they don't need any help or either worried what others may say or think about them; and overall, every solution that other hurting people advise aren't always the best advice on how you should go about things. Sometimes counseling is needed in order to seek the answers your needing. It's nothing wrong with seeking an outside source, and the information you share is "Withheld" confidentially. You don't have to worry about your business getting in the streets so others can have something else to share concerning you.

Some people have a hard time "Healing" only because they don't have the right support system, especially those that want a change or want to be healed. It's hard now days to share the things you're going through with people, because most of the times it's something negative they have to say; or either its wrong advice that someone has given to you, and it's not what you want to hear versus what people will tell you because they think it's what you want to hear. How can you expect "Spiritual Wisdom" to be shared with you when you're not willing to change based on the ideas someone is giving you instructions on what to try differently, in order to have a better tomorrow? There's so many people that's living their "Life" based on what they we're doing ten or fifteen years ago; and wondering why nothing has changed in your inner circle. …it's because you're doing the same thing other people have been doing for the last fifteen, twenty year!

Now how do you "Break" that chain of cycle? Remove yourself from those of "Negative" influences, and spend time alone to find out who you really are. You won't be able to touch bases on the good things within you until you are able to be strong alone and by yourself. When you can spend time with yourself and "Reflect" on the person in the mirror, then you would know exactly what "Sophia" means. Aren't you tired of "Blaming" other people for your problems and downfall? Why not take time to reflect on that person inside of your own skin—and that person is you! Why keep allowing yourself to keep going in circles repeatedly, and pass by so much time in your "Life"?

Are you that sure of yourself that you have time to waste in the things you do? How can "Life" move differently if you choose not to walk differently? "Sophia" is so sick of those that are "Willingly", and those that want to do better; but making up excuses for their self.

Not too many people who "Sophia" can say have spoken "Positive" in her "Life"; but she "Promises" not to hold back any information of getting started to enter in to the "New Beginning" of many people's "Lives"—that's what "Sophia" will not do. Many people will say they want to see you win but secretly and truly they don't, especially when you're a "THREAT" to the devils "Kingdom" to set the record straight in individuals "Lives". Do you know what damage a person can do when they're sent to correct you in order to help be an "Blessing" to you? Do you have any idea what you're doing when you help other people come out of "Bondage"? It's like you're "Destroying" the stronghold off of peoples "Life" in order to bring changes, and there eyes are open to see things they should have seen—in other words bringing "Clarity" to many people.

Some will accept, some people will not—so as long as you do your part to help someone, it's up to them to keep moving forward or not in order to receive their "Healing". You'll be surprise what people will think of you when it's coming from you to those that have talked about you so "Badly"; and they feel "Bad" when they have to come back to you and ask you for "Guidance" in their "Life" on "How" and "What" they should do. You should have no ill feelings towards them. You must keep on loving them and give them the advice they're seeking.

Just because other people wanted or wished you had failed doesn't mean you should want them to "Fail." You see, other people words and thought about "Sophia" and her "Children" was "Ineffective," so why should your "Strength" from other people be a "Weakness" to your spirit? Their words have given you "Power" to "Stand" and help other people. Like a scripture in the Bible says, what the "Devil" meant for "Evil," "God" sure enough does know how to turn it around for your good! To those that understand the words in the "Bible," they understand "Sophia."

How do you "Not" know that you had to be "Mistreated" and "Overlooked" to the "Core," and cry out every tear that you carry deep down on the inside for many years in order to see a change. What if it takes you to be "Wounded" for many years in order for you "Soul" to be "Shaken" to be a "Witness" to yourself to where you had no idea who you really are anymore? "How" do you "Not" know that "Life" had to look so "Dark" for you in order to see the lesson learned in your situation? "How" do you "NOT" know many people have to witness you at the "MOST" lowest and "Vulnerable" times in your "Life" in order to see the move of "GOD" in your "Life", and in order to see you as a different person and "Light" to their answers?

"Sophia" has sure felt every feeling. There's no way you could have told her that there was a way out with darkness coming from the "left and right", "north", "east", "south", and "west" in her "Life". Many obstacles have tried to "Stop" "Sophia", but sure enough she thinks about many people in slavery today and put herself in their shoes, as if she's witnessing their strength in the "Battles" they fought...in order to get through as a "Strong" "Black Woman" with much "Determination" and "Strength" so as to push past every

"Pain". There is "HEALING" in the world for everyone; but the question is, will you be open to receive?

That's where your journey begins, when you can be "Honest" and open to admit something is "Wrong" with you and you have no idea where to start. "Try" something "New", get out of your comfort zone, do you even if you have nobody else. Continue to stay in your own lane and continue to be "REAL" with yourself; and being "REAL" with yourself is "NOT" being connected with people that want to see you "SUFFER". Be "TRUE" and "FALL" back from them. "Sophia" sure had to learn that it's more "PEACE"; and you really see people for who they really are, and how they feel towards you. …but all at the end, it's a "BEAUTIFUL" situation when you can kick back and look at all of your "Accomplishments" you've made with "NO Man" approval and "Lack" of "Support" in the "MIDST" of your "Breakthrough" and "Healing", and you still maintain your "FOCUS"!

"Sophia" would tell herself "DAM" you're an "AMAZING" "Woman"! So why not continue to motivate others to keep on dreaming and make time for their self alone so you can be alone. Let your tears "FLOW", and don't care to "WIPE" your tears away. Let your "ANGELS" keep them in a bottle! It's time for you to go get your "HEALING"! It's time

Sophia Long

to "LOVE" yourself again! "Sophia" would say "GO GET
WHAT "GOD" GOT FOR YO

CHAPTER 5

WHEN SISTERHOOD BEGINS

When does "Sisterhood" begin? In order to have "Compassion" for other "Women" you "MUST" experience being "BROKEN" to the point that it has left you with "Great Compassion" to have "LOVE" for "Women." "Sophia" look at "Sisterhood" in a totally "Different" way. The "Women" she lost dug "DEEP" in her heart, which it took a few years after her "Grieving" stage to actually see what happened in her "Life", in order to understand the "Real" purpose in her "Life."

What message was "GOD" trying to send her way for her "Life." "Sophia" knows that she can't be connected to just anyone, knowing God has a "Big" plan for her "LIFE." That's why she's more "SHOCKED" at the few "Women" that have caused "DISAPPOINTMENTS" in her "Life" in the recent years when it comes down to "Handling" "God's" business. "Sophia" don't have any room nor time to waste for any "Riff-

Raff" in her inner circle. But "Sophia" sure has learned that "GOD's" business is serious to her and she "THANKS GOD" for the "Women" she lost, for her "Dedication" on why she's doing the things she's doing.

"Sophia" "Must" be "Honest", she can't "STAND" the few "Women" that she recently had to let go of in her past; because of their "Dishonor" and "Disloyalty" in which wasn't pleasing in the sight of "GOD." Let's not get it "Twisted," "Sophia" is "Kool", but "NOT" that "KOOL"! Neither will "Sophia" play with you or anyone else; "TRUST" she has far enough on her plate—more than others on an everyday basis.

So what we're "NOT" going to do is act as if "Sophia" takes doing something for "GOD" so lightly. Now if you promise "Sophia" a "Happy Meal", and you didn't buy the "Happy Meal" for "Sophia", then "Kool", she can handle that one and take that easily on the chin with no problem. But, where "Sophia" (and many other people that have had a relationship with "Sophia") sure does "NOT" use the word "Friend"…"Sophia" will use it because "Sophia" knows that the word "FRIEND" has *been* lost it's value a long time in "Sophia" sight.

But to those few "Women" (they know who they are) who act as if they touch and agree and wanting to do work for

"GOD" "Kingdom," and "Promise" you what they're going to do, and "SWEAR" they're going to do what "GOD" wants them to do, they're "DEAD" wrong for setting that type of examples to other people. That's the "Difference" between "SOPHIA" and other people; "Sophia" does her best to do what she promises people, even when she may forget she reach out and let them know she haven't forgotten about them.

What comes with building a "Sisterhood"—it doesn't come easy and neither is it supposed to be "Comfortable" when you're sharing yourself with other people. But, you should also be able to "Stand" when something is right and wrong. People have no idea of what they can feel deep down on the inside. It can be conviction of how they know they have done you wrong and still not apologize to you. But it's ok, "Sophia" knows she has done other people wrong as well and "NEVER" had a chance to apologize to those she hurt.

We have to learn that a load can be "LIFTED" off our shoulders if we just tell the "TRUTH" about what we're feeling on the inside, with the things we're battling on the inside in order to help someone else heal. "Sophia" is now speaking to the "WOMEN." How can you say you want to help other "WOMEN" but you're "Discrediting" other "Women" and putting them down? How can you say you want to be a

Sophia Long

"Blessing" to other "Women" but your cursing them all at the same time, wishing ill upon their "Life" all at the same "DAM" time? "Women," how do you set a "Positive" example when you're "MESSY", all at the same "DAM" time? It's either you're going to be a "Positive" or an "Negative" influence on other people's "Live's"; and if you say in one breath that you're an "Positive" influence in other people's "LIFE", make sure your character lines up with the way you talked. If you're ditching out "NEAGTIVITY," your character speaks for itself in your attitude.

The way you carry yourself, people will notice if you are the person you claim to be. You can't hide behind any fancy clothes and jewelry and think nobody sees you. You present yourself better when you can deal with "Real-Life" situations under pressure. You know it's not easy when you're used to acting out every time someone says something about you or mention your name in a negative way, or better yet, spread lies. "Sophia" had to go through a season of biting her tongue and "Standing" against people in a positive way! It's hard when your used to "Cussing" everyone out and make sure they feel every word in the "MOST" "PAINFULEST" way.

...I mean so "crucial" when a person would want to "DAM" near "SHIT" on them self, and be ashamed at the things they've done, and make them "Regret" every word they've spoken against you. "Sophia" didn't care how she made a person feel on the inside; but as she "Matured" she tries her best to use "Clear" words and understanding, with such a "DEEP" message, to where it leaves conviction in people's heart because of the "Truth" she knows about them. "Nobody" like correction of their own wrong doing. Some people just can't handle the "truth" about their selves, especially if your repeating back to them the words they've said to you. They "HATE" it and try find ways to find the arrows that's already "Broken" to try to harm you with some "Hurtful" words, which their plans shall fall once again.

People need to "STOP" trying to act as if they "STANDING" up and doing the right things, and "STOP" calling "GOOD" evil and "Evil" good! Especially the "WOMEN", come on… We "MUST" do better than that! Many of us already have a lot on our plate just by being an single "Mother", and you still want to "Hate" on another "Woman" that's going through "HELL" and "Hot-water," and you have the "AUDCAITY" to try and plot and take another "Woman" down that's in the same "predicament" that you're in. "Shame" on you "Women"! HOW "Dare" you say to the next "Woman," you want to see them "Succeed," and you're "SPITTING" on them.

"Sophia" would say "SHAME" on you for allowing the "DEVIL" to make you look like a "PLUM" fool! Who are you "WORSHIPPING"? We can't be serving the same "GOD" when using His name in "VAIN", being on a serious mission before him. "NO," that's not; so we're on two different accords! There's no way "Sophia" can and will "STAND" for that type of "Behavior." We're "Not" going to put "Sophia" in the same category with "Hating" other "Women." Now let's be "REAL! If anything, we as "Women" should be ganging up on the "MEN" rather! Women should be drying each other tears from one another faces, "Praying" for the "Men— whatever the case. What we're "NOT" going to do is act as it's ok to do the next "Woman" wrong on "Sophia's" watch! To be "Honest," that's not of "Sophia"—not in this "Life" today!

When "Sophia" lost the "Women" dear to her, it made her even the more "Compassionate" with "Women". When "Sophia" lost the "Young Women" that was "Dear" to her it left a hole in her soul. "Sophia" have had to face her "Sister's" children "Face to Face", without trying to shed a tear in her eyes, and all at the same time looking at her "Sister's" children in the face—knowing it wasn't her own strength that kept her standing.

Looking at the children faces as "Sophia" prepared dinner for her "Nephews" in the kitchen, as they share with "Sophia" how she reminds them of their "Mother." "Sophia" silently cries on the inside and "Laughs" out loud, to allow her sister's children to continue on bringing interest into their conversations. As "Sophia" remembers the "STRUGGLES" with their "MOTHER," and remember how they both had hard times being "Mother's" at so young, and the old memories flashes across "Sophia's" mind, hearing their "Mother" "laugh", and visualizing her shedding "Tears" all at the same time.

How do you keep your composure on your own? It wasn't "Sophia", it was "GOD" that kept His arms around her as she was dying on the inside. Truly "Sophia" just wanted to "Collapse" in the middle of the floor and ball up crying. "Sophia" had to continue to "Pray" in silence. You know us "Women" are "Sensitive" when feeling "Pain." "O," it was hard listening to my "Sister's" children talking about their "Mother"! That's one side of the story, and another beginning of another friend "Sophia" called "Sister." It feels "Good" when you know you've been "Good" to someone, and her family "Acknowledges" you in your "Sister" obituary. "Wow," and people want to take 'Sophia" like she's a "Joke" when she holds "WOMEN" dearly to her heart that don't have their "Mother."

Please don't come for "Sophia" with "No MESS" about a "Woman and her children"! This "NOT" that! It's a "Different" "Life" and season for "Sophia," and "MOST" "Women" still need to be seasoned. Those that think they there with "Sophia," and "TRULY" "Not"—"NO" "Sweetie", you have a lot to learn, aiming for "Sophia" at her direction. Things are "NOT" so "SWEET" when coming to talk to "Sophia" about "Nonsense" concerning "BROKEN WOMEN"; better yet, people are saying their "BUILDING" for "God" kingdom, and are really "JEALOUS" of the "Women" they're "Helping," or supposed to be "HELPING"— come on now! "BOW DOWN" Satan, with your "LIES" and "Schemes"! "Sophia" isn't missing out on "NOTHING" when dealing with nonsense "CHURCH FOLKS." This is so "NOT" that—not on "Sophia" "watch" or "clock," just like that!

"Y'all" "FAKE" "PREACHERS" and "Teachers" can stay away from "Sophia" with all the "Non-Sense" and "Drama." "Sophia" don't want her hands in "Nobody" else's

"JUDGEMENT" nor "DRAMA." "Sophia" will leave that up to the "Teenagers" and "Immature" folks. Do you really think that "Sophia" has the time in her schedule to play with some "Grown adults" when she's still "HEALING" from the "Women" she has lost? "NO MA'MA," "NO-SIR," "Life" isn't a game with "Sophia"; so please "Stop" assuming she wants something to do with you and his "DELVISH" things he's using up to get "Sophia's" attention—because in "Reality," it's "NOT" working.

"Sophia" no longer "WORK" for the devil, he's *been* dead to "Sophia." "Sophia" has let "GOD" arise in her "Life"; so "Ladies," please "Stop" being so "MESSY." If you see someone in need, and you're someone that's talking about another person clothes, "PLEASE" go buy her an outfit to help the situation. "Sophia" don't want to hear it! "LIFE" is "REAL"! It's too many people on the "BURGE" of "BREAKING" and they feel as "SUCIDE" is the only option. "Check" on your "STRONGEST" people, they need the same thing you need…a "Hug," "Encouragement," it doesn't matter how strong you think they are, check on them.

"Sophia" can't "STAND" messy people—"MAN" or "WOMEN", family, whoever—she's tired of everyone being "NASTY" to those that's going through "HARD" times.

What's "FUNNY" about someone living in a "SHELTER" or "SLEEPING" in their car with their children, as if you haven't been there? You *already "FORGOT" where you came from*? Please let's not let "Sophia" get *too* "DEEP" with the things she knows about people, but won't share a name because she's "NOT" "MESSY." Please "STOP" getting the words and "MESSY" and keeping it "REAL" mixed up. Those words doesn't mean the same; so which "CHARACTER" are you?

"SHAME ON" trying to "BREAK" the next "WOMAN," when "MOST" "MEN" have "TREATED" many of "US" "WOMEN" like we were "SHIT" coming out of a "HORSE'S" ASS"—let's not forget that! "LOL," Yeah, "SHIT" is funny but so "FUCKING" "TRUE"! Remember that the same group of "WOMEN" was crying along with you and sharing their stories about how they all got "CHEATED" on,...and then some of y'all "Women" act as if y'all "NEVER" shared the same "BLOOD," "SWEAT," and "TEARS" all in the same "BREATHE." But the person that was the "MAIN" leader in the "GROUP" get attacked and "Rejected" the "MOST" because "LEADERS" "LEAD", and should always tell the "TRUTH" anyhow.

If you have been in "Sophia" shoes you will understand where she "STANDS." "Sophia" had to face another

"Woman" who she called "SISTER", that was "MURDERED" child, "Face to Face"; and her child call "Sophia" "MOTHER". It's "HEARTBREAKING," knowing she's the only child, knowing she have neither parents, and they both have "Fallen" in the category of "MURDER" victims; and people think it's "O.K." to play games with people souls that's at "STAKE." They think they doing you a "FAVOR" by lying on you, saying as you're a "Suspect," as if you did "Wrong" by saying "NO" that's "NOT" right—"that's "NOT" at all of "GOD," that's "NOT" what we going to do! "GOD" only knows what "Sophia" means when she say it's no game. "GOD" is about to hold many people accountable for their actions.

When you know your calling is to help people, let your attitude be "JOYFUL" in the "LORD", as if you're a "CHEERFUL" giver. When you give to other people, make sure it's nobody else's business what you do, and please make sure it's "Pure" from the heart when you give. Don't you know people know when you're "NOT" giving from your heart, from your hand to their hands? "Silly" rabbit, do better than what you're doing if you're planning on being a "GREAT," "POWERFUL" "WOMAN."

Represent "GOD" now for all other "Women," treat your neighbor right, and if you see another sister in need of a car, if you're able to afford it, put them on top and buy that "Single Mother" a car! Why be afraid to be a "Blessing" to someone else? If you have the money to buy that "Single-Women" a car go buy her a car. If you have the money to pay that single "Mother's" "light bill," go pay her "light bill"! How do you not know if "God" is sending you family that you "NEVER" had, in order to give the "Love" you "Never" had, and you didn't know how to receive the person or people He sent to "LOVE" on you?

How do you know if you missed your opportunity to have a "Sister" you "NEVER" had because of the "HATERED" that had been stored in your "HEART" all alone, and you just wanted to have someone to "BLAME" for your "BAD" attitude and errors you've made; but in "HONESTY," we all have to be held "Accountable" for our own action in the things we do.

What are you doing in your communities in order to bring about change? What are you teaching the "Young girls" in your community? Are you setting examples before them? Or are you talking about the "Young girls" as well, with your old "self-righteous" self. Or could it be you're laughing at them as well, because they're "sixteen" with two babies, with two baby daddy's that's not even there, and forgot you were once them? How are you bringing about the change, and reaching the next generation if you're busy putting them down?

The world needs us "WOMEN" to be "STRONG" for them; because what "GOD" has put on the inside of us, that's "NOT" in "MEN". At this point, I don't care who don't believe in "GOD"; but this is now the time to keep mentioning Him. "Sophia" is "Not" ashamed to say she "LOVES" "GOD" and to tell people when they're "WRONG." "Sophia has learned a lot in her "LIFE," and she has "Grown" a lot because of her past experiences, and the cards she was dealt which had "BROKEN" "Sophia" spirit down into pieces.

The pieces of her "Heart and Soul" are still "HEALING"; but "Sophia" won't "STAND" for anything. She's "OLDSKOOL" and from "Detroit, Mi", from the "Eastside" where her "Mother" raised her; but the streets made her become who she is today, and the people in the streets have taught "Sophia" the "Biggest" lessons in her "Life"—stay strong and "Correct" her "Wrongs," and give back to those that's in "GREAT" despair because of the things she endured at so young, and how she was treated so "Badly" by those she "TRUSTED".

"Sophia" has always wanted to help other "WOMEN" because of the "PAIN" and "Struggles" she has been through.

"Sophia" always knew she wasn't like other people and she knew that one day she was going to help "Women," even if it meant sharing her story to other people! ...especially moving to "Georgia"... "God" has opened so many doors for "Sophia," and she has met so many "GREAT" people from celebrities, she has spoken to many young people, many opportunities have come knocking at "Sophia's" door; but some she had to turn down. "Most" of the time, "Sophia" was offered money and she wouldn't take it—especially when it came down to speaking to the young people; because "Money" isn't everything to "Sophia."

Sometimes you have to do what you're called to do and don't expect anything in return, because in return, "GOD" rewards you all in the end. "Money" isn't everything! It's ok to say "NO" to people even when they offer you something, even when you may need it. Sometimes it's ok to turn "Money" down. You have to know when to take from people and when to give, when to say yes when to say no.

"Sophia" just want the "Women" to "Love" one another and stick together and know the "REAL" "Women" will "Always" take a "STAND" and "EMPOWER" one another. It's time to "POUR" into one another and "BE REAL" with one another, and be "TRANSPARENT," and "Be a "Blessing"

75

towards one another! "Sophia" is routing for every "Woman" that's "REAL," and "Understand" the "REALNESS" she brings and what she "REPRESENTS" in the things she "LOVES" to do.

There's too much going on in this world today to be "MESSY" and "DEGRADING" to one another. It's time out for that, and if you're "REAL" like you say you are you shouldn't want to be connected with people that's "Beneath" your "Standards." You should "ALWAYS" be connected with your own kind. If you're about "BUSINESS," stick with those that's serious about business! We already know "GOSSIPERS" stick with "Gossipers," and "Gossipers" doesn't flow with "Sophia." "Birds" and "Bees" flock together! Anyhow, "Sophia" enjoys everyone and she hope to see "MORE" "Positiveness" in each individual, especially the "WOMEN"—we got this!

"Sophia" really hopes everyone understood the message she was saying, and that it's ok to be "BOLD," and "NEVER" back down when you know you're "RIGHT"! Many people won't be able to "HANDLE" you, and "SOPHIA" sure is used to the "HATERS"; and if you don't have any "HATERS" that means you're "NOT" doing your job right! Anyhow, I wish everyone well, and may "Peace" and "Blessings" be unto you all! …know that "Sophia" means well to all, even the "HATERS" with "Backlash."

Let "NOTHING" stop you in this season, because this "SHALL," and Will" be your "WINNING" season; and give your "BEST" in all that you do! …and let "NOBODY" STOP YOU! THIS IS FOR ALL MY "REAL" "SISTERS" EVRYWHERE! IT'S OUR SEASON TO SHINE!! "MAY GOD BLESS EACH AND EVERY LAST ONE OF YOU"! IT'S TIME FOR THE "DEVIL" TO BE BROUGHT TO "SHAME"! "PLEASE KEEP YOUR EYES AND EARS OPEN TO THOSE THAT'S TRYING TO BE CLOSE TO YOU"!

Made in the USA
Columbia, SC
06 May 2021